Atlantis

Atlantis

LAUREN EDEN

ATLANTIS

Self-published by Lauren Eden.

Cover art and illustrations by Jessie Spencer of Sage Rider.

laureneden.me

ISBN-13: 978-1976253836
ISBN-10: 1976253837

For Mum
my first home
my Atlantis.

Had I not been born
into this world of you
I would've thought
your breath was the wind
your voice was the sun
and the sway of your womb
was the sway of the sea.

I would've known love.

Only love.

Contents

Blue

There once was a boy
who fell in love with
the blue of my eyes

but then he saw the ocean.

It was time that took you away from me

we had too much of it
to think
to languish
to fade

nothing ever stays the same
but what if too much of it does?

How long before the sea
is no longer seen as sapphire or indigo
but blue
simply blue

cherished not for its whimsical waves
but for its lost treasure
sunken to the bottom?

Just as I look into your eyes
and try to find myself in them somewhere —
forgotten.

Dive my deep sea diver!
Swim my virile voyager.

I beg you re-discover me
beneath these ruffled covers.

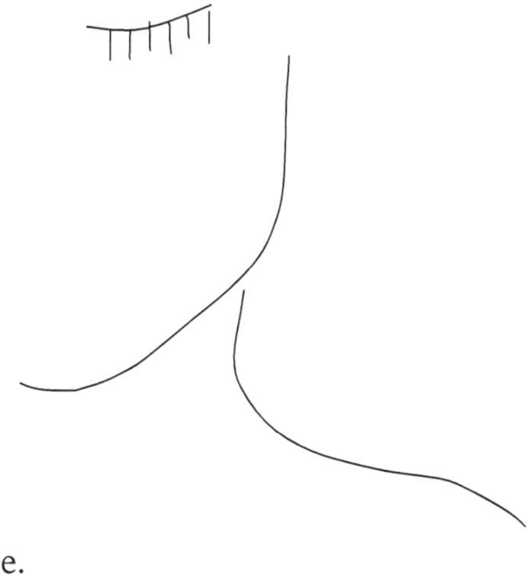

His eyes wander
to the right of me.

What's left
is no longer
worth seeing.

I am half
the woman
he fell in love with

and I'm breaking
into quarters.

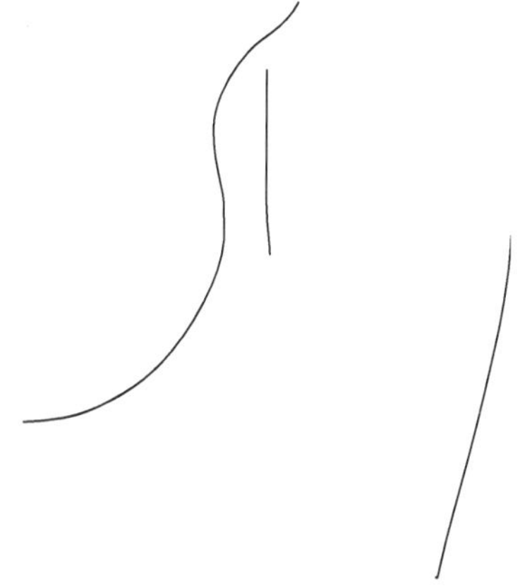

There is something
about the evening

the way
the sun leaves

the way
the sky bleeds

and the moon
and I grieve
for something
we once had

and can't quite
remember.

I am more than
this housewife
in suburbia

locked behind
a sticky fingerprinted door

wearing
a lipstick-red smile
dazed eyes and
impeccable manners.

I used to be a hurricane.

I used to be a revolution.

What they always said
was good for me
is killing me slowly

it's just a dreamier
more alluring death

like a water ballerina
dancing her final pirouette
down the drain of a bathtub.

All the flowers picked

words written
kisses kissed.

What are we
my love
but a slow
enduring river
wishing it were a sea?

A water out of luck

shaken out its salt

waves ironed flat
like a bed sheet

feathers leaking
from our pillows
like teardrops

flying back
to the birds
they came from.

It makes me weary
to ask for a love
that should flow
naturally like water

softly

simply

trickling down
to all the places
I need it to go.

I reined myself in
so many times
for the world
I forgot the freedom
of my toes

while my desires
ran rampant
like wild horses
through my bones.

They don't tell you
that broken in
just means
broken.

For nine months
I slept beneath your heart
like a throbbing moon

beating to the tempo
of a lullaby I grew to

and in a trance
I've followed
the heartbeats of men
like tribal drums
mistaking their
rhythm for yours

sleeping on their chests

nails dug in tight

trying to find the heart
I wanted best

but the truth is
I always wanted
your heart best.

Oh mother
what have you done to me?

You're closing again
he says.

Like a flower
I say. *Not like a door.*

Delicate. Not slammed.

It's the same thing.

I feel death
stalking me
in the stillness
between my breaths

chasing
the last exhale
like a fox chases
the slowest lamb.

I wish
my heart
would fall into
his hands
as easily as
my breasts do.

It was like
not wanting to
wriggle out of
his arms because
I didn't want to
wake him.

That was what
it felt like to
fall out of love
first.

I know what my mother is thinking
when she looks at my face quietly

my wide-bridged nose
my blonde hair
my deep-sea eyes.

Your father won the argument.

My heart
rumbles
in the night
with a hunger
for a taste
it does not know
but knows
what it's not.

You took
your eyes off of me
and we shifted

and I existed
in your periphery
like a long shadow
in the corner

like the glimpse
of a lover's dress
before she walked
out the door.

I nearly died
having my son
and some days I wonder
if it would've been
a fair trade

two litres of blood

two

while my daughter
came clean out
still in her sac
like a fish trapped
dreamily
in its bubble

and I wonder

how some people
can be made so
perfectly for us

and others
not.

I mourn
my softness
like a woman
mourns her milky
young flesh

now milked.

We stopped kissing

afraid

that if we opened
our mouths wide enough
our secrets might
fall out.

The tears leaked
softly from my eyes
like flower petals

and I swear
you would've smelt jasmine
had you put your head
close enough to mine
which you became
fearful to do

you've always
feared for your life
around a sad girl
as though she was
crying a monsoon.

We talk of tomorrow
before the day is done

and that is how I know
we are running
out of love

faster

than we are running
out of time.

They argue
the moon is male
but only a woman
still shows up each night
a mere shadow
of herself.

I am so close
to who you
want me to be

so close

you wish
I was farther.

When you tell yourself
that everything you have
is *good enough*

you have swallowed
the voices of everyone
you are trying to please.

He hugs
the back of me
like he has caught me
running and is not
letting go

and that is how we sleep.

That is how we live.

He sips me as he needs

politely
like a weak cup of tea

absently
as he reads the newspaper

one hand light on my hips

a quick kiss

a shallow swish
between his lips
as he progresses
through the day
to the harder stuff

seeking those
he'd rather swig

women
not at all like me.

Peg by peg
I hung up my desires

watching them dry
on the clothesline
before folding them
neatly into piles
in the linen cupboard

where all good wives
keep them.

I wonder often

was it my eyes
that wandered

or you
that wandered
from my sight?

Oh how many nights
I've laid in bed beside you
wishing that everything
in this room was enough.

You don't need a man.

My mother
said these words to me
more times than
I heard her say
Clean your room.

She knew it was men
that made the most mess.

Tears

how dare you
be so light and clear

when I have
the wildest colours
of hurt inside me.

I had never
loved a boy
who didn't
love me back

until I had a son.

I will never be

one
of those beaming
shiny faces like
little suns
people revolve
around.

I am a sunset
smeared
across the sky
like the blood
of something
that once lived
boldly.

I tell my kids before
I put them to bed

Your mother was
a fairytale once

but her story ended
when she was just
about your age

although she did
begin again

on a new page

in a different tale

but I don't tell them
it was not quite
the same.

I would watch you drive

not able to take
my eyes off of you
while yours
stayed unwavering
on the road

not knowing then
it was how our lives
would always follow

me looking at you
looking straight past me.

I get it.

I'm polarising.

I am soft
feminine flesh
floating through the room
with the grace
of a feather

and on the inside
as hard as the egg
that did not crack

a dead bird
that never felt
what it was like to fly
because its mother
never kept it
warm enough.

I cry

but the kids
cry louder.

They always
cry louder.

11am in suburbia
and the street is filled
with beautiful empty
lavish homes

vacant of people
out all day to pay
for these
beautiful empty
lavish homes.

The sky

a fist
clenched of stars
like silver coins.

I search the soil
for seeds of you
that won't be sown.

O greedy hand of fate
I have come too late

death blows below
the belt of Orion

where due north
points south like
a spinning-bottle mouth
open for a kiss

our lips miss

time pauses

the moon yawns.

We make love
like we're about to break

like building sandcastles
on the shoreline
surrendering
to the inevitability
of ruin

you
holding my face
in your hands
one last time
before it washes
away.

I disappear downstairs
to the spare bedroom
where it's dark
like a dog finding
somewhere quiet to
die alone.

I don't want him
I say.

You rock him in the doorway

my bags packed.

I don't want him.

I hear a whimper
I've never heard before
tremble at the back of my throat

a short quick sound
like a stone thrown
in a ululating stream
my heart skips.

I cannot shake
this suspicion

like rotten fruit
on the highest branch

but will I not become
just a fool to temptation
as you have

biting into all the wrong things
to prove I am right?

I wish
my daydreams
weren’t so vivid
they made life
look like a picture
that's been hanging
too long in the sun.

They will sense
the gaps
between us

and like snakes
through the wire
slink with sex

with apples
in their eyes

the colour of
their sundresses.

The truth is

I stopped inviting them
over for dinner
because I couldn't
stand to watch them
hold hands across
the table when we
let go.

We walk through the crowd

his grubby hand
reaches for mine

You're the best mummy
he says. *I don't want you*
to get lost.

I listen to the two men
in the front of the line place their order.

I'll have a tall skinny mocha
skinned lady who is better in bed
than in the kitchen.

I'll have a grande
pair of Reebok Pumps
that I can take off in at any time.

I'm next.

I'll have what they're having
I order.

The young girl behind the counter
puts her hand to her pretty pink mouth
and gasps.

Oh no. You cannot do that
she says. *This one is for the ladies.*

She passes me a menu.
The options take up a quarter of a page:

Venti housewife
Espresso mother

I smile as tightlipped
as her pre-birthed pussy.

I'm not sure I can stomach either of them.

Waves

Don't make waves
they say

but the sea has not made
a single one

moving only in reaction
to the moon
the winds
the tide.

It is you who stirs me.

I think
if I love them
hard enough
I will soften them

but though
water will wear
down rock

rock will never
be water.

When I tell you
I'm trying

what I'm really
saying is

I'm trying
so hard to fall
back in love with you
and I have no clue
how to.

I search your face
for a semblance of you
but you have changed

shifted
like the world
on its axis

little by little

less by less

as I lean
into your light
and see only shadow.

He talks
about the strippers
he saw last weekend
in front of his wife

not noticing her sip
her wine faster.

You see it's
harmless fun
really

other women
taking off their clothes
for your husband
when you get undressed
each night quickly
in the dark.

I try to keep
the doubts at bay
as I watch you
slip away.

I'm not
you tell me.

I'm not.

But I've studied you
for years.

Don't you think I know
when someone else
is reading my
favourite book?

If it is peace
that I seek

why does
my wild heart
feel like it's
playing dead?

She tells me she's leaving her husband.

I tell her I've been thinking about
leaving mine.

She stirs a second teaspoon
of sugar into her coffee.

You remember Marie?
The one with little Louie?
Well she's also thinking about
leaving her husband.

Are all married women thinking about
leaving their husbands? I ask.

We look at each other.

Suddenly neither one of us
is feeling quite so rebellious.

I stoke our fire lazily
with new lingerie
on a body you've seen
a thousand times before

knowing
I'll only inspire
one lick of a flame
you'd rage with
a new woman

wearing old lingerie
she's worn a thousand
times before.

I will not be
reprimanded
for failing to keep
my feet firmly
planted on the ground.

I keep telling you
the world has not
stopped spinning
since the day
I was born.

There are women my age
starting to knit and crochet
and I'm still fantasising about
fucking their husbands.

I remember waking
the morning after
my wedding day
feeling like I'd been
hit by a truck

ribs bruised

shoulders tender
and stooped

and it took a moment
to realise it was the weight
of my wedding dress

the weight of marriage
had crushed me to the point
I struggled to move

and I wasn't yet
one day married.

You spy an elderly pair
down the street ahead of us
holding hands and coo

That's going to be us one day

assuming old Beryl and Fred
have been romancing since 1939.

You don't know that they've
been together that long
I say. *Maybe they only met*
last week at Bingo.

You look at me.

You don't know me anymore.

Like thread

we weave in
then out

we stay
we leave

we stay
we leave

for that is how
two fabrics
not cut from
the same cloth
love

trying to make
something
out of the best
they've got.

He's there again.

Tuesday 11am

table to the farthest left
beside the wood-fire and
stack of magazines
beating the lunch rush-hour.

No wedding ring.

There's either
something wrong with him
or he is smart

very smart.

I imagine he has
a roulette wheel
of women he spins
each night

each number lucky

one tried and trusted word
exquisite bouncing
around them as they giggle.

They want to be the lucky one.

Men don't say exquisite these days.

I cut my hand on us

the shattered glass
of our wedding picture
you put your fist through
last night

and I am still
picking out shards
of heart from my hair

spitting out syllables
of your surname
like broken teeth.

I walk the tree-lined streets

pass the straight-teeth fences

the freshly cut lawns

and trip on the top step
before I get to the door

blood on my knees

skirt up around my thighs

and I smile.

I smile.

I've seen my mother and father
in the same room no more times
than I can count on the two hands
they made me.

I don't know how they talk
without my mother knotting her arms
like rope in front of her chest
trying not to laugh at the jokes
my father tells to undo them.

I don't know how they sat
curled up together on the couch
watching TV

the look on my mother's face
as she fixed the collar on his shirt

how they kissed

what it looked like
when they loved each other.

If they did.

I'm not sure
I was made with any.

Every time
I ignore that
cold heavy feeling
in the pit of
my stomach
it ends up
swallowing me
first.

I am thumbtacked to you

like just another
half-hearted promise
to stay

and you are the board
hanging around waiting

predictably

for me to pull the pin
again.

Your hands
find me in the dark

our 4am tryst
between the sheets

two strangers
acquainting to lovers.

I'll give you my best side
if you can give me yours

because in the morning
when we wake
our backs will be turned
to draw.

I walk into the bar with you

one of the two men sitting
at the table across from us
looks at me and says to the other

When you have a wife
you're either the luckiest
son of a bitch or
the unluckiest.

I mull over his words
as I sip my beer

not caring which one
of the two categories
they've put me into.

I already knew.

You were the luckiest

then you ran out of luck.

I like anger
in my sex

the kind of fuck
that leaves evidence.

He used
gentleness
against me
so my mother
would never
know.

You tell me
I mustn't remember
how much you loved me
in the beginning

and I tell you
that is the problem.

I don't know how to forget.

This is what we've come to

scrambling through
the rubble of us
trying to decide
what to save first

and saving nothing.

I pretend I can't see him

watching me
blow dry my hair
in front of the mirror
as I tilt my head to
show him the slope
of my neck

and inside
I am trembling

one wrong move
and I fear he'll fall
out of love with me
again.

I made my peace with men
when I grew a boy in my womb.

How could I fear something
I could make?

She tells
her life's story
to the cashier at
the supermarket

this little old lady
with mauve-coloured hair

toes stretching wide
in her slippers
like sighs

tired of answering
fine

when she really wasn't fine.

I watched the moth
on the window
press itself
against the glass
at the reflection
of the moon
and I wanted to ask

What made you settle
for a reflection?

What made a mirage
of what you really wanted
enough?

I looked at the man
sitting next to me
on the couch
and I knew the answer.

I'd been smelling
petrichor for days

waiting for
the final downpour
that would wash us
clean away.

They tell boys
there are plenty
of fish in the sea

but they
never tell girls
about all those
fishermen.

I was the rope
my mother and father
played tug-of-war with.

Forgive me
for not learning
how to share myself
without putting up
a fight.

I've always thought
the infinity symbol
looked like a noose
for two.

For what it's worth
he begins

I don't love her
and I won't.

These words
I've been dying to hear
have come too late

each word rattling
like a penny inside me.

I am empty.

It's worth nothing
I say.

Nothing.

Women
are as powerful
as a loaded gun

as powerful
as prayer

the way
they bring men
to their knees.

Her short
chubby hands
find my hair

my tears
leading like rivers
to places I hope
she never finds.

Good girl
she whispers.

I said my goodbyes
on the curve of your neck

sharp kisses hidden
in whispered regrets

all those times
I will never forget

counting your eyelashes
as you slept.

(They never added up to infinity)

I want to know the exact moment
you fell out of love with me

the day
the hour
the minute
the second

your hands

where they
were positioned

on your temples
in your lap
holding your beer?

Were they in mine?

Fingers receding
like the shoreline

while I choked on
all the words
I couldn't say
dry like sand
at the back
of my throat?

The tide turns
your head to the side

facing shore

the shock of the wall.

A whisper creeps
between us like a child
carrying a nightmare

I can't do this anymore.

You roll over
to face me like
a wave into the rip
of our sheets.

I'm careful not to fall back in.

We weep
a calm sea.

The boat begins to rock.

Tide

We cry salt.

We were made to heal.

With the microwave
in the trunk

toaster
strapped into
the passenger seat
where you used to sit

apron strings
jammed in the car door
dragging along the road
like a *Just Married* in reverse

I drive away from
the domestic bliss
my fore-mothers
strived for before me.

I loved you
in a thousand
different ways
and lost you
in one.

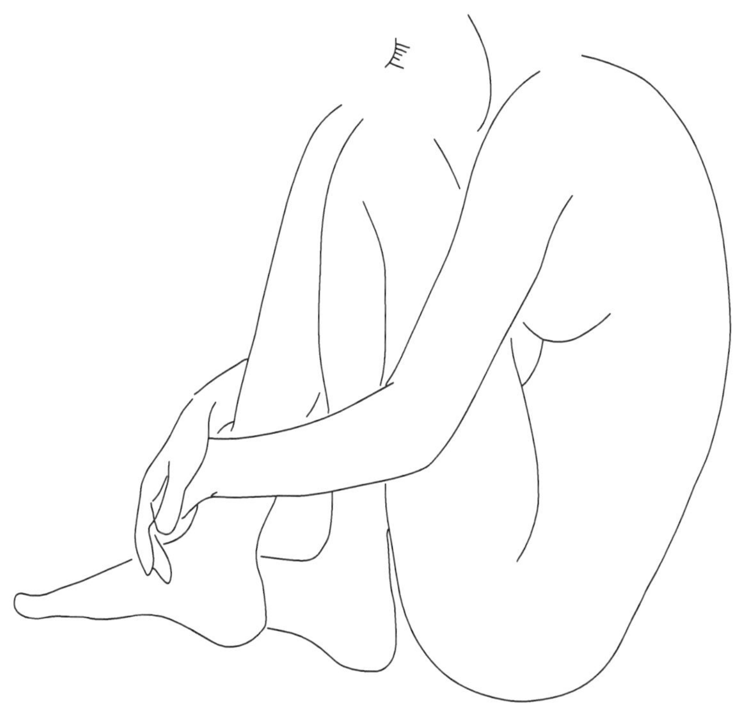

It was not the sound
of your shoes
shuffling the dirt
into new patterns

nor the sound
of your hands stirring
in your pockets
after they left mine

it was the swing
of the gate wailing
a ululation of all
the women in me

sharing
the burden of loss
only one man
could bring.

We withered
like leaves

brown-speckled
and hard like
old hands
we'll never hold

falling too soon
and too fast
like cards
that never knew
when to fold.

I might
never again feel
the veins tangling
like vines down
the branches
of your wrists

but I will remember
those moments
when you could've sworn
it was my blood
bleeding through
them.

Nowhere you are not.

That is the Hell they don't talk about.

It isn't fire
or a wide gaping mouth

it is an empty bed
and your coffee mug
sitting untouched
on the table.

I reach for you
and my hand falls
through the air
empty and slow
with the heaviest
weight of nothing.

It's the plans
that cry at night

every night

standing
in your doorway
like a woken child
from a dream
you need to put
back to bed

and it's the journey
down through the cold
bones of midnight
you fear you won't
come back from.

My eyes wander
from small thing
to small thing

anything at all
in the room
but him

his eyes
a litany of blue

hands in the safety
of his pockets.

Do not reach for me
I beg under my breath.

I know how your touch will undo me.

Sometimes
loyalty is
just a word
we use to
shame people
into returning
to us.

Heartache
is a dead fish
in an ice bucket
frozen with
memories of
the ocean.

When every angry word
has been spat in your face

guilt smothered
like a murder across your mouth

disloyalty bruised blue

you don't look
like love anymore

you look like hurt

and strangers will
cross streets to avoid you

friends will no longer call

because they fear
you will hold onto them
with those sad curled fingers
and you will not let go.

I am still
on my knees
in the debris
of our love

while you
are in a bed
making more
with someone
else

and I wonder
if you even
needed to
grieve for us

or if your cry
into the curve
of her throat
was enough?

I wish I could've said
My door is always open for you

but now I'm older
I know better.

That is how
the draft
gets through.

We draw up
our family trees
and don't talk
about the ones
that fell like leaves

or the branches
that were cut off

or the fact
that we are not
even trees at all.

There were
always too many
wandering feet
than there were
buried roots

and that's just
the way it is.

I look at my phone
at his olive branch message

I hope you're well

implying I wasn't before

that my hurt
was a symptom
of the kind of hysteria
a woman is prone to

and I want to tell him
No. I'm not well. I'm still sick.

Sick of the shit
humans do to each other

lying through their teeth
because their own truth
is hard to swallow.

No. I'm not well.

I'm hysterical.

We became hard work.

How could I compete
with these women
who looked like vacations

with cool-sea eyes
and skin hot like
the kind of sand
that sticks to you?

I wish healing
didn't feel like
just another way
to forget you

and if it didn't

I just might.

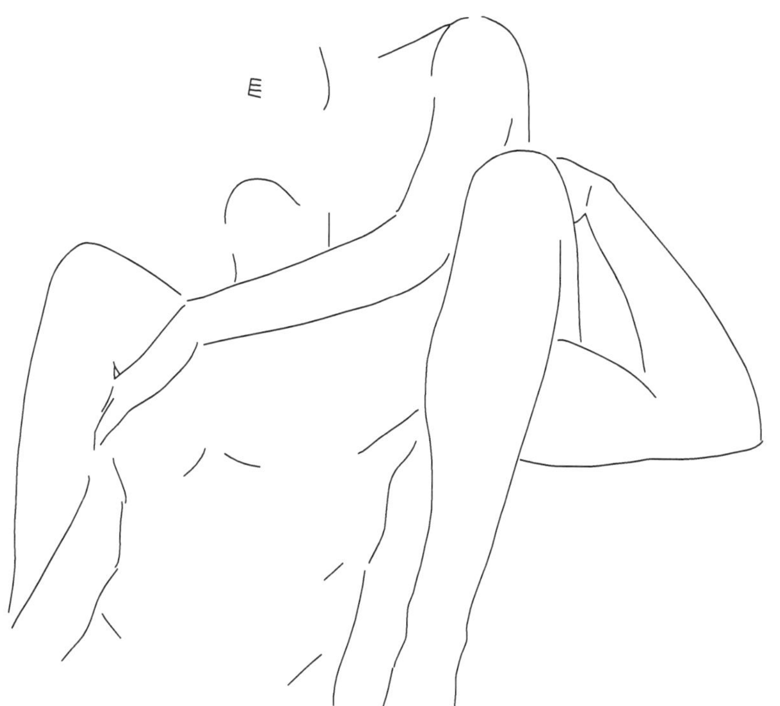

I shook you out
of my hair
like seawater
but the salt remained

embedded

the way pain clings.

You were the one
I wanted most

to be the one
I wanted most

but you were
the almost moon
a moment before
it was full

and I was the wolf
that howled too soon.

I cut my hair short
as a *fuck you*
to the men
who pulled my
long hair hard
to keep me still.

I've made peace
with *almost*

that space
between arm span
and reach

that nearly

kind of

more or less

never enough
fill of you
that never
quite pacified
the rumble in me

like waves
I can now fall asleep
listening to.

I took myself out on a date today.

We did coffee.
We did cute conversation.

I told her she was beautiful
in all the ways that mattered.

I laid her down
on her king single bed
with the cherry blossom sheets
and made love to her.

She came. Twice.

I promised I would
never leave her. Ever.

Then I found some spare time.

I called you.

I talk
to the moon
and she tells me
it's okay to change.

Please excuse me

I am still
heaving up
the morals
I was force-fed
as a child.

It might
take some time
before I find
what makes me
hungry.

I made up
so many worlds
in my head
I forgot which one
I lived in.

She was born
inside her Atlantis

her underwater world
still intact

before the nurse
wielded
her silver weapon
with her cold
strange hands

bursting her bubble —

her paradise
a puddle
on the floor

a paradise
she'd spend the rest
of her life looking for.

An ache
where the feeling
used to be

like the pain
of the womb
contracting
where life
once lived.

Bundle up your hurt
and try swimming
with it in the ocean.

You will soon see
how easy it can be
to let go.

It was your hand
sitting at the sill
of my collarbone
like a bird at a window
waiting for it to open
that made me see
that I was closed.

How did I not see
that I was closed?

One day
all of those wounds
will open up again

but this time
you'll bleed love.

Happiness
[hap-ee-nis]

verb:
1. Watching kids eat watermelon.

It was on the delivery table
under a stark
white light
that I truly saw
the cycle of things.

Pain was not
a symptom of death.

It was a sign of life.

She thinks
if she steps
on the cracks
she'll break
my back

not knowing
that daughters
can do a lot more
damage than
that.

Resist your urge
to connect my dots.

I am a beautiful
mess of stars
rebelling against
the constellations.

I'll admit

it sweetened the blow

to find out
the one you left me for
left you
and now we're
both alone

you
inching closer
with your scent of charm
and I leaning
back into myself

resisting

what I once found
irresistible.

We stuck to surface streets

I never felt invited
into your home

you had things in there
you didn't want me to see

things
you had locked away
for so long perhaps
you'd forgotten
what was in there

but I was a curious child

always peeking through
the keyholes of you.

In the quiet
slumber
of my skin
is peace
offering herself
to me.

I make love
to passing men
with my eyes

my blinks
the clicks
of all the doors
I close behind.

Don't be a stranger
I plead

but they never stop

just look

always moving
always leaving.

There is a quiet
tucked between
my bones that
unsettles me

like an empty street
you walk down at night alone

turning around
to see if someone
is following you

and the scariest thing is
no one is.

I expect love
to feel like peace.

I turn men
into gods

worship at their feet

and I feel nothing
but a sinner
when I feel nothing

nothing at all

just a few butterflies
inside me

when I wish
they were doves.

Be brave.

Fall like the rain
not knowing where
it will land.

I see them

these women

like lost pages
fluttering away
in the breeze

begging
to belong
to a story

wanting
to be read

before they've been written.

Love him like a sea

swim

letting
the ends
of your hair drip
in the memory

watery lines
down to the dip
of your back
where his mouth
drew you so close once
you almost cried
at the tenderness of it all

sweat into tears

salt into salt into salt

thrown back
into the sky
like stars.

You were never out of luck.

We made
daisy chains
in the sunlight
and I prayed
it would be
this simple to keep
two people together.

I would string up
all your leaves
if I could

wrap them around
your wooden neck
like a garland

weaving and weeping
weaving and weeping

singing eulogies
into the wind.

You will grow back
what you've lost.

You'll see.

They were not
just days that
passed between us

they were shifts

the hours
a tug in the other
direction of you.

Forgive me
for not falling
so easily back
into you today.

The door
of my childhood home
was always open

not to welcome guests

but to let the men
in and out with ease
while the women begged
on their knees

please

I'll try harder
I'll love harder
you can fuck me harder

thinking they had
all the power
to make love stay.

I am not my mother.

These five words
that have been
soaking in my mind
finally arranged in order
and hung out to dry.

I. Am. Not. My. Mother.

No. The cycle of suffering ends here.

I blow up a balloon
for my daughter and tell her
we're celebrating.

Maybe those same words
will leave her mouth one day.

I am not my mother.

And we will blow up
another balloon.

We will celebrate again.

I once fell in love
with a fisherman
who kissed me quick
then threw me back in
like I was one of plenty

and then there was
that sailor who knew
I was the sea.

We made love
again
in the water
under the bridge

heads bobbing
like two promises
rising to
the challenge
of forgiveness.

Let go.

Sway
upon the sea
that brought you
here to me.

What is
meant for the shore
is meant for the shore

no less

no more.

End

SCHOOL OF FISH

Exam Paper

1. When did you drown?

____

____

2. Who brought you back to life?

____

____

3. Whose lifeboat did you climb aboard?

____

____

4. Did you swim? On whose wave?

____

____

5. Can you float?

____

____

About the Author

Lauren Eden is a writer from Melbourne, Australia, who began her writing career posting her daily musings on life and love on her popular Instagram account @ofyesteryear

Lauren's first poetry book, *Of Yesteryear*, was published in 2016 and was hailed for its short, clever and snappy lines.

The writing of *Atlantis* quickly followed after a brief love affair with a roaming and very charming neighbourhood cat of the same name, whose current whereabouts, despite Lauren's paper trail, remains unknown.